THE COMPLETE GUIDE TO EMAIL MARKETING

BOOK VI: USING EMAILS TO INCREASE LOCAL AND ONLINE SALES

by Gini Graham Scott, Ph.D.

Author of 50+ Business and Self-Help Books
Email Marketing Company Director
for 13+Years

THE COMPLETE GUIDE TO EMAIL MARKETING

Copyright © 2017 by Gini Graham Scott

TABLE OF CONTENTS

INTRODUCTION: THE MANY WAYS TO SEND EMAILS 5

CHAPTER 1: DECIDING WHAT EMAIL TO USE 7

Setting Up Multiple Emails 7

Deciding On the Your Email Platforms 8

Using an Email from a Website 8

Using an Email from a Phone Company 9

Using an Email from a Free Service 9

Choosing Your Email Name 11

Using a Personal Name 11

Using a Company Name 12

Using an Industry Name 13

Using a Made Up Name 14

CHAPTER 2: SENDING EMAILS TO INDIVIDUAL DECISION MAKERS . 15

Creating a CRM System 15

Setting Up Your CRM System 16

What to Include in Your CRM System 17

Using CRM Software Programs to Track Your Progress 18

The Advantages of Using a CRM System 21

Other CRM Systems 22

Using a CRM System 27

ABOUT THE AUTHOR 29

INTRODUCTION: THE MANY WAYS TO SEND EMAILS

There are many ways to send emails – among them are sending out individual emails, using a platform to send recurring emails, and sending out bulk emails, which can sometimes be personalize or not. Other considerations include what email to use, whether to personalize the email, and whether to include graphics or links and how many to use.

Thus, deciding on the best approach to sending an email can be a complex, in addition to deciding what to say. Which approach to use depends on what you want to say and who you want to target. Knowing the full range of possibilities can help you choose which approach is the best, depending on your message and target.

As a rule of thumb, keep your messages on a topic to a particular email address, so you maintain a brand consistency.

But once you start engaging in an email exchange with an individual after sending a bulk email, you might ask selected individuals to switch to another email used for a continued conversation. This way you can distinguish these emails from all emails in your initial mailing, which has received responses from those interested in learning more and other types of responses, including those who want to "unsubscribe" and automatic emails from those who are away or gone from the company.

CHAPTER 1: DECIDING WHAT EMAIL TO USE

You may already have an email that you use for everything. It may be an email tied to your website, such as john@yourdomain.com or marysmith@yourdomain.com, or an email with one of the popular free providers, such as gmail.com, hotmail.com, or yahoo.com.

Whatever your current email, set up multiple emails and where possible, don't use a free email account, for reasons to be discussed. Preferably, use an email linked to your website or linked to your phone or cable company, such as john@comcast.net or marysmith@att.net.

Setting Up Multiple Emails

Multiple emails are sometimes linked to multiple websites which feature different products and services, although you might use multiple emails for other reasons, such as doing promotions for different purposes.

Having different websites can be an ideal scenario for creating different emails for each website. This way it is clear what service or product you are promoting, as featured on the website, and the recipient can always go from your email to your website to learn more about you, your company, and other offerings.

Using an email linked to a website can give you more credibility when contacting a person who doesn't know you, because an email with your domain name looks more legitimate than an email from one of the free services. Having multiple emails for each website contributes to your credibility, too.

Another reason for having multiple emails is so you can keep track of the different people who respond to different orders. While you can create folders in an email and move your emails about a product or service there, this can be a time-consuming operation. Also, you may lose track when you engage in an email exchange with different people in the same email about different topics. And it may be confusing if a recipient changes the subject line to more closely reflect what the conversation is now about. By contrast, when you have multiple emails for different products, services, or types of conversations, you can more easily keep the emails on a particular subject together.

Having multiple emails is also a good idea when you are testing different approaches, prices, subject lines, photos, and other changes. This way, all the responses to one email show a different type of response from those who respond to another email. You can vary your email name and provider for different purposes, too.

You can also prioritize how often you check different emails, based on where you more often get emails, so you more frequently check the emails you use the most and spend less time checking the others. Then, check off each site as you do these check-ups to keep track, so you don't waste time with extra checking again, because you don't recall if you previously checked an email or not.

For example, I have about 25 emails, and check five regularly. I have some emails under my name, some under different company website names, and some are on gmail.com, comcast.net, and yahoo.com. And when I create new project with a new website, I sometimes use a forwarding email to an email I use more often. Because of the nature of my business, it makes sense to have these multiple emails for different products, services, and campaigns.

Decide on the number and type of emails that work best for you.

Deciding On the Your Email Platforms

However many emails you have, a key consideration is what platform to use. The major types of platforms are these:
- an email from your website
- an email from a phone company, such as Comcast or AT&T.
- an email from a free platform, such as yahoo, gmail, hotmail, and AOL (yes, there are still some of those).

<u>Using an Email from a Website</u>

Ideally, if you have a website email, that's a good way to contact people in an initial mailing, although you can easily set up a forward to an email you more regularly use, so you can more quickly see any of these emails. For example, this might be the email on your website when people contact you for more information (such as info@yourwebsite.com, contact@yourwebsite.com, or yourname@yourwebsite.com. Then, that email gets forward to an email you check every hour or two, so you can respond quickly, which shows you are very responsive and customer-service oriented – a big plus when you are trying to gain new business.

Using this website-based email is also good for an initial mailing to prospective clients or customers, since that looks more professional than if you use a free email or email from a phone company. You appear more solid and established, since you have a website. This web-based email also gives a new prospect a chance to go to your website and check it out, because that website is clearly indicated in your initial mailing, though you might later respond from your regular email.

You can also set up multiple emails from your website. Then, if you want to keep them separate, forward them to different regular emails. In fact, if you have multiple officials or employees at the company, forward these emails to each person's personal email and that person can respond.

Another advantage of a website email is it is less likely to be viewed as spam and rejected by the filters and spam bots on some email servers.

Using an Email from a Phone Company

As an alternative to a website email, or if you don't have a website, a phone company platform is a good second choice. This is less likely to run into email blocks than a free email account, but there are some limitations.

Based on my experience, you will only be able to set up a certain number of emails for each phone line (commonly 6 to 10 email accounts, as is the case with Comcast and AT&T. However, if this is important to you, you can always get another phone, and even if you drop that phone or that phone company merges with another, you still may be able to keep that account. For example, I still have my pacbell and sbcglobal accounts, though these companies are long gone, and I still have my att emails, though I dropped by second landline phone with AT&T.

Using an Email from a Free Service

Probably the preeminent free service email is Google's gmail, which is quick to sign up for, though with one caveat. Unless this has been changed recently, you need to have a mobile number where the service can text you a message, and you can only use that same mobile number for a limited number of emails (about six in my experience). So you can only have a limited number of emails associated with a particular mobile phone number. Also, certain generic names can't be used, such as when I tried to create an account for emailmarketing@gmail though I could add a number such as emailmarketing17@gmail or emailmarketing20@gmail, though all of those were taken. But emailmarketingconnection was okay, and this time I didn't get a request for a phone text confirmation, perhaps because this was linked to a series of gmails with the same account.

A feature on many of these accounts is you can connect them to your mobile phone, so you can access your email on the go. And many accounts, such as gmail and yahoo, enable you to move email contacts from other accounts to your new one.

However, one caution in using free emails is that you may run into certain sending restrictions and blockings by servers, because many free accounts have been used for spam. I discovered this while running and later working with an email connection service for over 13 years. About 4 years ago, email protocols changed, so it was no longer possible to send out emails with yahoo.com or aol.com accounts through third parties, such as by using special software and an SMTP server to put any email in the send and reply field, so the email appeared to comes from that email and any replies would go to that email. However, emails from certain platforms like yahoo and aol get blocked, so if you try to send out such an email, you will get back most or all of those emails. For example, if you send out 1000 emails from this third party software and SMTP set up, you may get several hundred emails back, and others may be deleted.

So far it seems like gmail is accepted. But others may not be, so if you plan to use a free emails with a third party mailing service, check to make sure your mails will go through.

The other major caution in using a free email is the reaction of the recipient getting an initial email from you. The recipient may take your email less seriously than if it comes from a website domain, or even from a phone domain, because anyone can easily open up a free account. Thus, the recipient may be more likely to see a pitch for something as an Internet marketing scam or as spam.

However, you might be able to override any such concerns with a very specific subject line about your topic rather than a short and general promotional message, such as "Great New Money-Making Opportunity" or "Discover the Secrets of the Internet Marketing Millionaires." This problem of thinking your message is spam is less likely, too, if your email is associated with a website domain, since this gives you more credibility at the outset. This is the case, since a person can immediately check out that domain, whereas if you send a free email with a link to a domain, recipients can more easily suspect that this is a link to a bogus site or the basis for getting malware or ransomware on their computer. So you have to be careful when using free emails for marketing pitches, especially with the recent news of Internet scams, spams, spoofs, phishing, and other ways of taking advantage of email recipients.

If you still plan to get a free account, I'd recommend gmail, since it is more widely used by marketing professionals than other free accounts. Plus, it is widely used by creative people and entrepreneurs, too.

Choosing Your Email Name

The next major decision in choosing your email name is whether to use your own name, your company name, or a name that relates to your business or industry. There are certain advantages to each, and this is why it may be a good idea to have multiple emails for different purposes and markets.

For instance, you might use a personal email to communicate with people after you have met each other, but use an email with your company name for an initial mailing, since it may look more professional or make it seem like you have a larger company, especially if you are using your name or company name with a phone company or free platform. But if you have a company domain name, using your own name can be fine, since that domain name establishes you as a company.

Since names aren't case sensitive, you can capitalize your name or company name so it more clearly stands out. Using all lower case is fine, too. Avoid ALL CAPS, however, since this is hard to read.

The following sections describe some of the times when you might want to use your own name, a company name, an industry name, or a made up name.

<u>Using a Personal Name</u>

An advantage of using your name with your website domain name is that it is easy to remember. This is particularly useful when you are using an email for referral marketing, after you meet someone at a networking event or get referred to someone. Then, your name provides a more personal touch.

Likewise, if you use your name with a phone company name or free email, it is more personal and memorable.

Using a personal name is also a good idea when a company has multiple officers or employees. In this case, it's good to have a format to identify everyone in the company, since prospective customers or clients can more easily reach a person, when they only have a name. They just need to apply the appropriate names format, as described in Book 4 on Finding Emails to Build Your Business. Common formats are these:

- First Name@companydomain (good if you want to be more informal and personal)

- FirstInitialLastName@companydomain (a more professional approach, used by some publishing and financial professionals)

- First NameLastName@companydomain (a widely used formula, which is ideal to promote both you and the company)

- FirstName.LastName@companydomain (another widely used variation on the firstname/lastname formula)

- FirstName_LastName@companydomain (another variation on the firstname/lastname formula, though less common)

Sometimes if you have a common name, it may not be possible to get that name by itself, when you use a phone company or free platform name. Thus, some individuals use a combination of numbers after their name, such as helensmith241@yahoo or dave.jones.452@gmail. In general, it's a bad idea to combine a name with random numbers, because such a name is difficult to remember and it looks unprofessional. It may be fine for communicating with friends and family members, but it's best not to use this name and number combination in business. An exception might be if you can get a numerical extension that adds a dramatic touch, such as helensmith01@yahoo, helensmith200@yahoo, helensmith2000@yahoo. But if possible, use an initial to distinguish your name which looks more professional, such as helenbsmith@yahoo.

Using a Company Name

When you initially approach a prospect for a cold call, it may be better to use a company name with a phone company or free email, because it sounds more professional and creditable. For example, the new owners who bought my Publishers Agents and Film Business decided to do. They selected pafconnections@gmail, because it makes the new company seem larger, just as I used publishersagents2@yahoo for over 10 years, when I was running the company and assisting the previous owners with writing and consulting for 5 years.

Also, using a company name works well if you are using a phone company or free email platform. Using that name helps to highlight the credibility of the company when you first contact someone, such as I have chosen here for the Email Marketing Connection (emailmarketingconnection@gmail, which is also the name of the Facebook group I set up.

Using an email in your company name is especially effective when your company name indicates very clearly what you do.

Generally, it is best to link together all of the words (ie: emailmarketingconnection) although some company owners separate them by dots, dashes, or hyphens (such as in email.marketing.connection, email-marketing-connection, or email_marketing_connection). But in general I would discourage using dots, dashes, and underlines, since people can forget which to use. Also, if you are choosing that option since the original name is already chosen, it may be better to choose another name or put "the" in front of the name (ie: theemailmarketingconnection) in order to get a .com extension, which is the most common and widely accepted one.

Using an Industry Name

Use an industry name if your company name doesn't readily convey what you do. This is an especially good idea if you are sending out emails to new prospects. This way in cold emailing, much like in cold calling, in two or three words you suggest what your company does, even before someone opens your email.

You can do this with your company domain name or with a gmail or other free account. For example, say you have a soul food restaurant, your company name is Soul Works, and your domain name is soulworks.com. Since it's not immediately clear that soulworks refers to restaurant serving "soul" food, rather than a spiritual practice involving "souls," the reference to "food" in the email name helps to clarify that. For example, your industry related name might be funfoodfacts@soulworks.

Or perhaps you want to reach out to another market, but your name isn't a good fit. An example might be a craftsman who is trying to expand beyond a local clientele, where his folksy name: "FurniturebyPhil" is great for his mostly small town and rural clientele. But now he wants to create wood furniture and other products for retail stores, like Ikea. Perhaps a name like: "woodgardenproducts@gmail" might provide an email that reflects Phil's broader scape for his product.

Using a Made Up Name

Finally, at times you might want to use a made-up name in your email, usually in conjunction with a gmail or free account. This made up approach might work especially well if you are in a creative profession or have a humorous book or product.

For example, one associate uses a term like "sunburst" to reflect his interest in using positive thinking to guide workshop attendees to the light. Another associate uses "astroflyer" to suggest his love of flying and his interest in aviation.

Such made up names can also be useful when you do a product or marketing test where different groups respond to different marketing pitches. Such tests, which involve slightly varying one or two components in an ad or sales promotion to see which has better results, help to show which is the best way to advertise or promote a project. Usually, you do these tests with two target groups at a time to see which approach performs better, and you can do additional tests to find the best approach. Then, you increase your promotional efforts using that approach.

CHAPTER 2: SENDING EMAILS TO INDIVIDUAL DECISION MAKERS

Some of the common reasons to send an email to an individual decision maker are:

- You have a product or line of products to sell to the company.
- You want to provide a series of services or do a project for the company.

In pitching a product, you need to have sales material and be prepared to demonstrate the product and provide cost and ordering information if the company is interested.

In the case of a service or project, you may need a proposal describing the service, deliverables, date for delivery, the cost of different phases of the project, and the like.

In either case, you often start with an email to get the decision maker interested in meeting with you, so you can present your product or service in more detail. Or you may initially meet the decision maker or be referred as a result of attending a networking meeting, conference, trade show, or other initial meeting. Then, you send an email is to remind the person of your meeting and seek a further meeting or phone call.

In some cases, you need to follow up with a video or PDF showing your product or service in action; in other cases, you may be invited to bring those materials to a meeting.

Creating a CRM System

To keep track of who you contact by email, phone, or personal meeting, it is important to create a CRM or Customer Relations Management system to keep track of the people you contact to when you make the sale or find out they are not interested, so you don't go through the process again.

Using a manual system, such as an Excel sheet, is ideal for individual sales pitches. However, you can increase the number of prospects you contact by using special software to send out and personalize your emails. Then, you follow-up individually later, as described in Book VIII on sending emails.

The advantage of a CRM system is you more easily keep track of the email pitches you send to decision makers at different companies. You track the emails you send, the response, the results of any follow-up meetings, and the cost of your average sales based on the time and effort it takes to make sale. This kind of approach is used by successful professional salespeople, and you can adapt it to be used both locally and in other states or countries.

Setting Up Your CRM System

Consider your CRM system like a spreadsheet which you carry around with you on your phone or set up on your computer, so you can record everything that happened during or at the end of the day. You can use a CRM system like a calendar to let you know who to contact to follow-up with on a particular day and time. You can also use the names and contact information for the people you meet to send them emails to follow-up or to send initial emails to start a communication and later follow up. In this way, you record everything as you move from the initial connection, referral, and lead to presenting your offer, any negotiation, and finally note when you close a deal.

Your CRM system should include the following columns, where you can add in this information as relevant in the appropriate column:

- Initial meetings, and where and when they occurred
- Rating prospects from a hot (5) to cold (1) lead or referral, so you can focus on the hottest leads first.
- Phone calls, and where and when they occurred
- Emails sent on what topics and when
- Meetings to present your project
- Follow-up calls, emails, and meetings
- Nature of opportunity for selling products or providing services
- Cost of the sale or deal

Include a section in your CRM where you can record the highlights of any conversation, phone call, meeting, or other activity. Also, include notes and follow-up plans. If someone refers you to someone else, make a record for that new person and indicate who referred you and whether by phone, personal meeting, or email. This way you can keep track of who are your best sources of leads and the type of referral they give you. After getting a referral, plan to follow up within two or three days, let the person making the referral know what occurs with that lead, and use the CRM to keep track of this information. To guide your further follow-up with each person, rate the prospect from hot (5) to cold (1). Plan any follow-up based on responding to your highest priority leads first.

A key advantage of the CRM system is that you can track your sales process, as you start with pitching your product or service in-person or by email. Then, as you get responses after your initial contact, you can increasingly zero in on those prospects that present the greatest opportunity for sales based on their level of interest and likelihood to follow through and buy.

The process works much like an online sales funnel, with certain prospect opting to continue through the funnel with one, two, or three upsells, while some decide not to go through the funnel at all. You want to assess how well that process or funnel is doing, and a CRM system can help you assess what you are doing right and what you should change to increase your potential for sales.

In contacting individual decision makers, start with the most promising leads who are either likely buyers or connectors, who can refer business to you, because they are top influencers in their field. In some cases, you might consider them "power partners," where you work together and refer business to each other.

While sometimes you can set up a meeting on the spot, a more common scenario is to exchange business cards, or at least get their business card so you can follow-up, because if they just take your business card, often they will not contact you. Should they claim no business card, offer to write down or have them write down their name, phone number and email on the back of one of your business cards.

However you get their card or contact information, note what they may be interested in. Then, add them to your CRM contact sheet, along with information about them and their rating as a prospect or source of referrals. Then, follow up with an email or by phone, and decide what to do next, based on their level of interest. While you should plan to follow-up with your highest priority leads first, follow up with everyone over the next few days. If you have less than a dozen or so contacts, you can use individual emails. With more contacts, use an email system that lets you personalize the email using the software and email server approach described in Book VIII.

What to Include in Your CRM System

Whatever CRM system you use, add in the relevant columns for adding information, comments and tips about following up with that person. Preferably use an email rather than a phone call for your follow-up, even with local contacts, since many people don't like to get random calls from people they don't know or have just met during the day. They find such calls disruptive, or you may get caught up in a conversation with their receptionist or assistant. By contrast, when you follow up by email first, they can review their emails when they are ready to look at them and respond. Whichever you do, enter it into your CRM system.

The main categories to include on your spreadsheet, some of which have already been briefly described, include these:
- Name
- Company
- Type of Business
- Phone

- Email
- Address/City
- Best Method of Contact
- Common Connections
- Level of Influence (1-5)
- Level of Interest (1-5)
- Potential Buyer/Referrals to Others
- Special Interests/Hobbies
- Comments
- Type of Initial Follow-Up
- Date of Initial Follow-Up
- Results
- Any Additional Follow-Up
- Date of Additional Follow-Up
- Results
- Plans for Meeting
- Date of Meeting
- Results
- Future Plans/Developments

You may find that other categories are relevant for you, including adding even more follow-up categories, if you are dealing with an especially expensive or complicated product or service. For example, some business associates report they commonly have four, five, or six or more meetings before finally landing a million dollar project in the housing industry. By contrast, others pitching less expensive products or projects, such as installing a floor or selling jewelry at a house party may only need 1 or 2 follow-up calls or meetings to make a sale or set an appointment to sell the product line to a group. Talk to others in your industry to determine what is most common.

Using CRM Software Programs to Track Your Progress

To illustrate how a CRM program might work, here's Pipedrive, https://www.pipedrive.com , which is recommended by some top salespeople. One of the advantages of Pipedrive is that it can synch your email account with the system, and you can send emails through Pipedrive which will be incorporated into the system. For example, you can list your leads, note when you make contact by phone or email, and when you have scheduled a follow-up meeting. If you make a proposal, you enter this into the system, note when you enter into negotiations, and indicate if you make the sale.

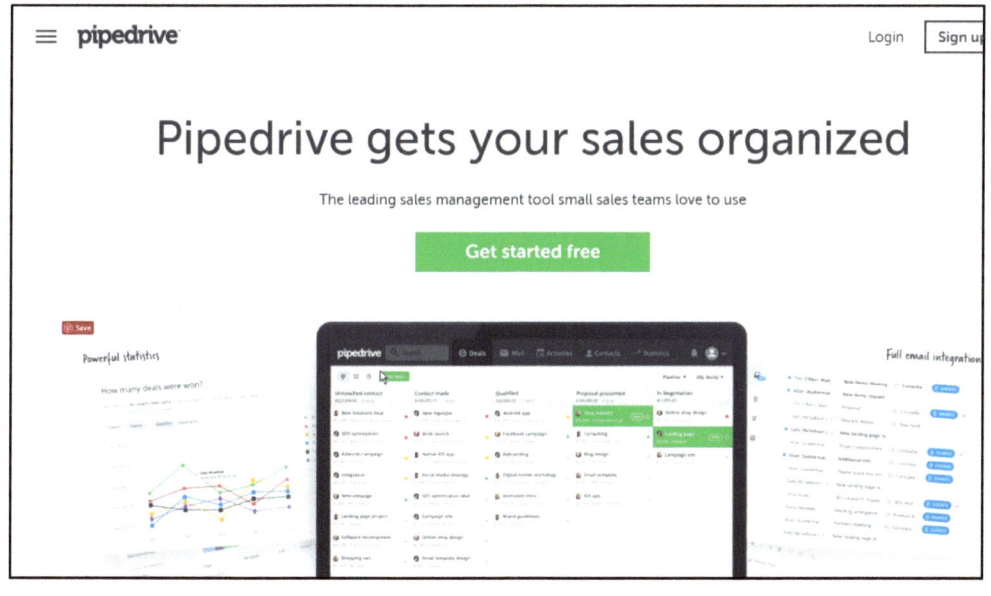

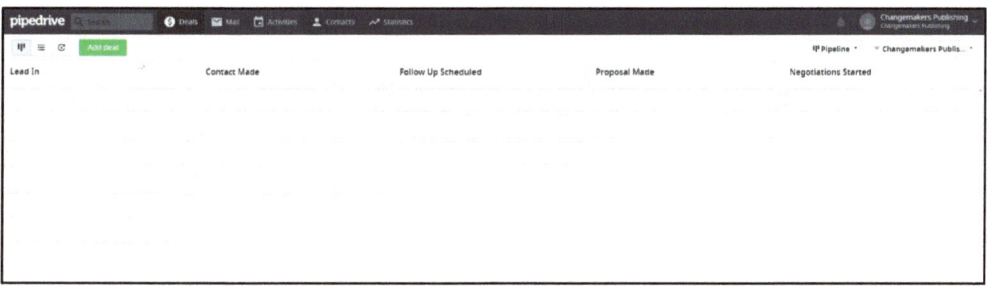

The system also keeps track of the results of following up on a lead. To do so, the system tracks when you make a call, have a meeting, send an email, complete a task, or otherwise follow through until you make the sale or don't.

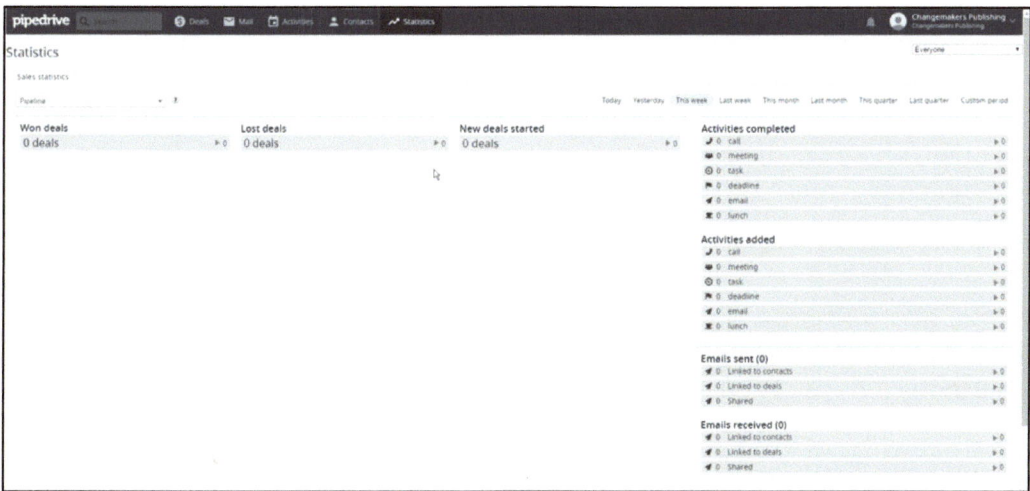

It includes a calendar so you can schedule an activity. Additionally, you can indicate who the activity is linked to, such as who referred you, what organization they are connected to, and what kind of deal you are discussing. For each activity, you note if it's a call, meeting, task, deadline, or email, and you can enter notes about that activity. As a result, when it comes time to place a call, send an email, have a meeting, or just have lunch, you know what to do.

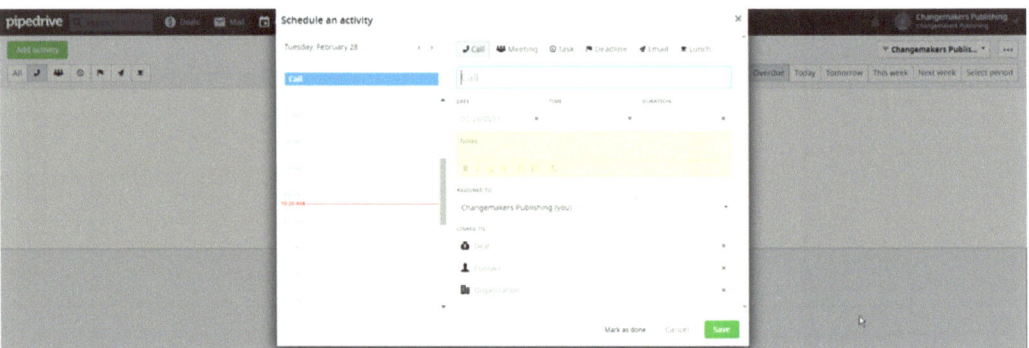

For example, on the following form, you can see how I entered a few activities for a call, sending an email, and having a meeting.

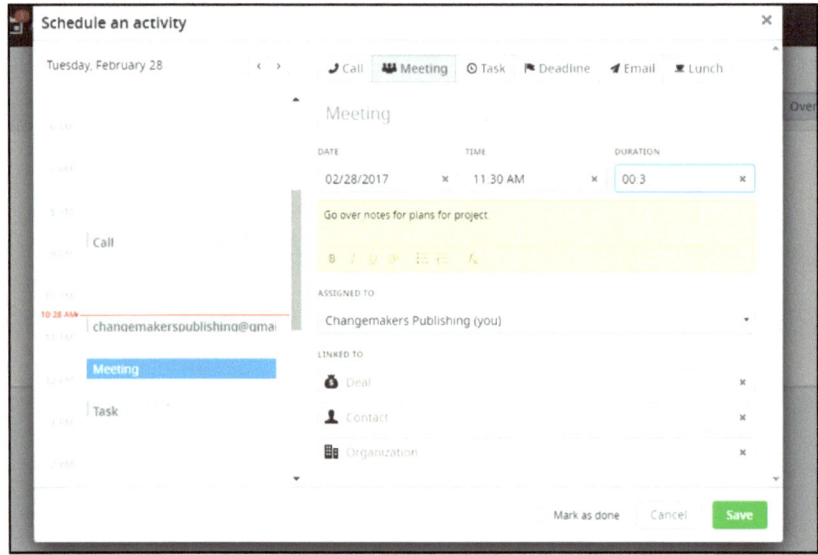

Later, you can see your stats for your deals, activities completed, deals lost and won. Obviously, I don't have any stats, since I'm just using this to demonstrate, but you get the idea.

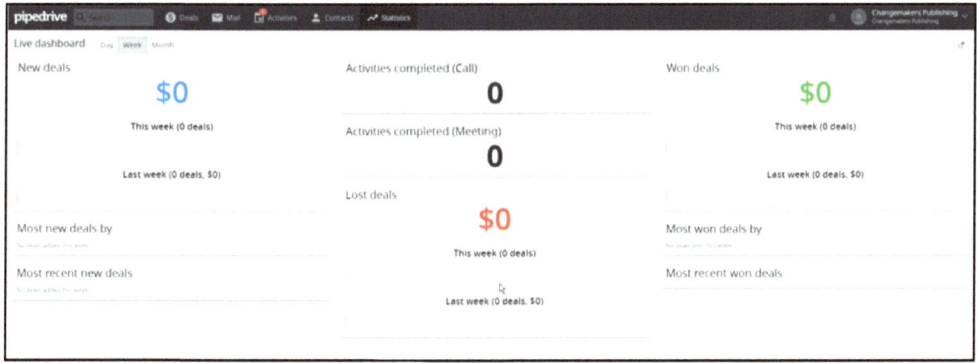

<u>The Advantages of Using a CRM System</u>

An advantage of using this or many other CRM programs is that CRM systematizes the sales and marketing process, including how and when to send emails to initiate a stage in this process. As a result, you are more effective in what you do, leading to more deals and sales.

Moreover, you can synchronize when to send out an email with all of the major email providers, such as gmail and Yahoo, and any cloud-based email services. Also, you can enter information about the main points discussed, when to follow up with a call or email, and the results at each stage of the process.

This system can also assess how well you are doing in monetary terms, so you can see what's working and the value of doing that. Say you usually earn about $2000 a week. If you find that by increasing the number of contacts you are meeting and emailing by 10%, you increased your earnings by 20%, that's a $400 value for a small amount of additional time to send a few more emails or make a few more calls. Then, if you get even bigger deals due to your extra efforts, the value you have gained increases much more.

You can use it to further chart your progress based on the dollar value of each deal and how likely it is to close, so you can prioritize where to focus your attention. Suppose you have a $20,000 deal with a 10% likelihood of closing, that's a $2000 value; whereas a $10,000 deal with a 40% likelihood of closing is a $4000 value. Knowing this, you should put more effort into that $10,000 deal. Of course, you have to accurately estimate the probabilities and the value of the likely deal for this approach to work. Moreover, as you move along through the sales funnel, the probabilities will change as will the value of the deal, so the deal value becomes greater because it is increasingly likely to close. Accordingly, you should put more effort into projects that are further along in the sales funnel.

For example, your $10,000 deal might now have a 60% likelihood of closing after you send some follow-up emails to schedule a meeting, and then follow up by email with a memo on the major deal points discussed at the

21

meeting. Then, if the other party asks to schedule another meeting, the probability might climb to 80%, so your work on this project is now valued at $8000. By contrast, your $20,000 deal might be moving through the system more slowly, so it's value is only 20% or $4000.

On the other hand, if you don't do anything to move a deal along for a few days – unless the other party has asked you to delay further conversations for a couple of weeks – the probability may drop. Thus, in most cases, these changing probabilities indicate that you need to do something to activate any deal in the pipeline, say every four or five days.

For example, one good way to keep a deal active is to do something to provide more value to show how you might help the prospect gain even more. For instance, you might send the prospect a summary of some relevant facts that show the value of acting now to complete the deal.

At the same time, if the deal seems stalled for a few weeks, the CRM system can remind you to make other contacts or follow up on other contacts already in the system. In this way, you get a series of deals working their way through the system, along with reminders of actions to take once you reach certain milestones, such as sending a first follow-up email after one week; sending a second follow-up email after three weeks, and so forth, until you schedule another meeting or two and close the deal. Or alternatively, the system can help you recognize that a deal isn't going to happen, since along the way you see clear signs of a lack of positive responses from the prospect.

You can also add in activity reminders on the day or night before for the following day.

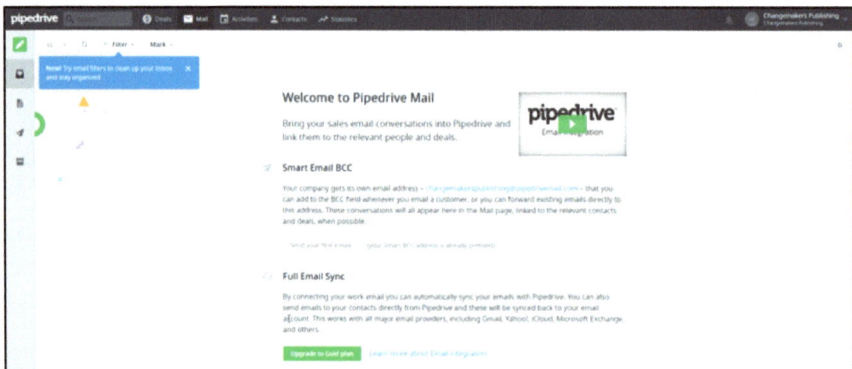

Other CRM Systems

Pipedrive is just one of many CRM systems. I used Pipedrive to illustrate, since it was recommended in one of the email marketing seminars I attended. Also it can be deployed on a computer, since many of the other systems are only available on the cloud or a mobile device.

That being said, the top 10 CRM software programs are the following according to Capterra (www.capterra.com), a major source of business software products. All of them include contact management, customer support, email marketing, interaction tracking, and lead management. They are listed according to how they can be used (1) computer, cloud, and mobile device; 2) cloud and mobile device; and 3) cloud only.

Computer, Cloud and Mobile Devices

Bpm'onlineCRM https://www.bpmonline.com/crm-products

Cloud and Mobile Devices

Insightly https://www.insightly.com

ProsperWorksCRM https://www.prosperworks.com

Marketing360 https://www.marketing360.com/small-business-crm

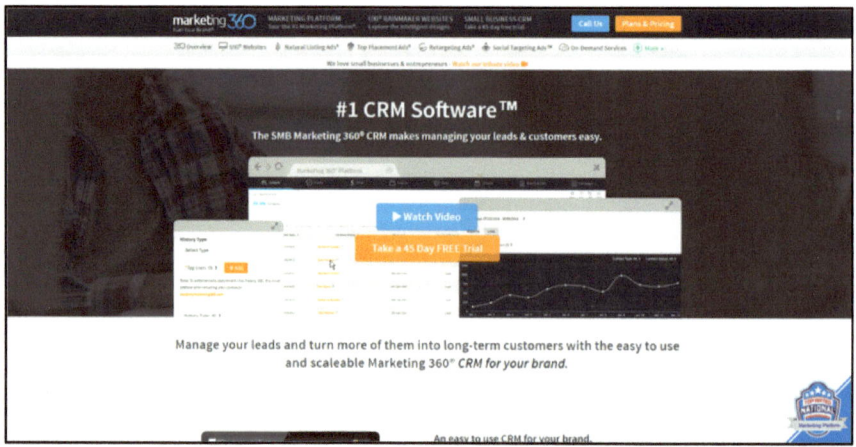

PipelineDeals https://www.pipelinedeals.com

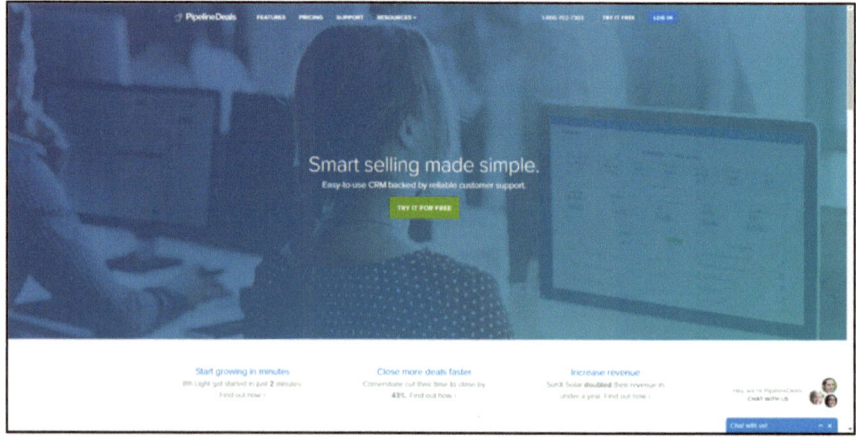

Desk.com https://www.desk.com

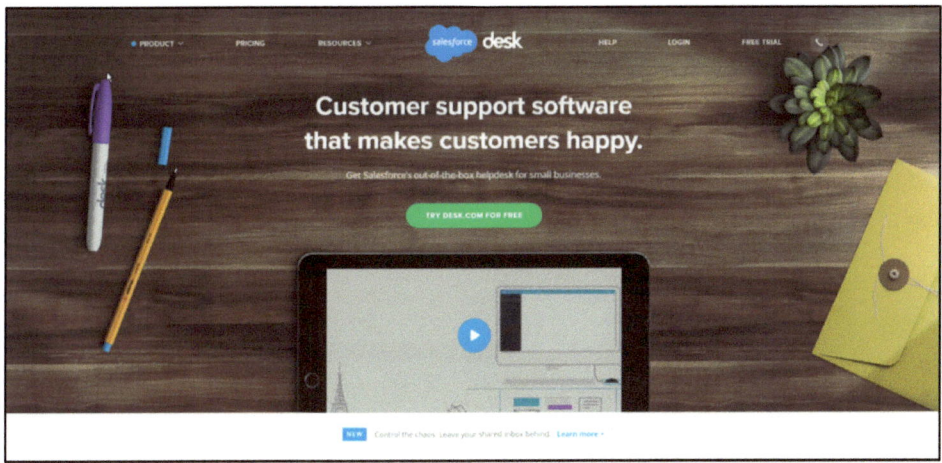

Base https://getbase.com

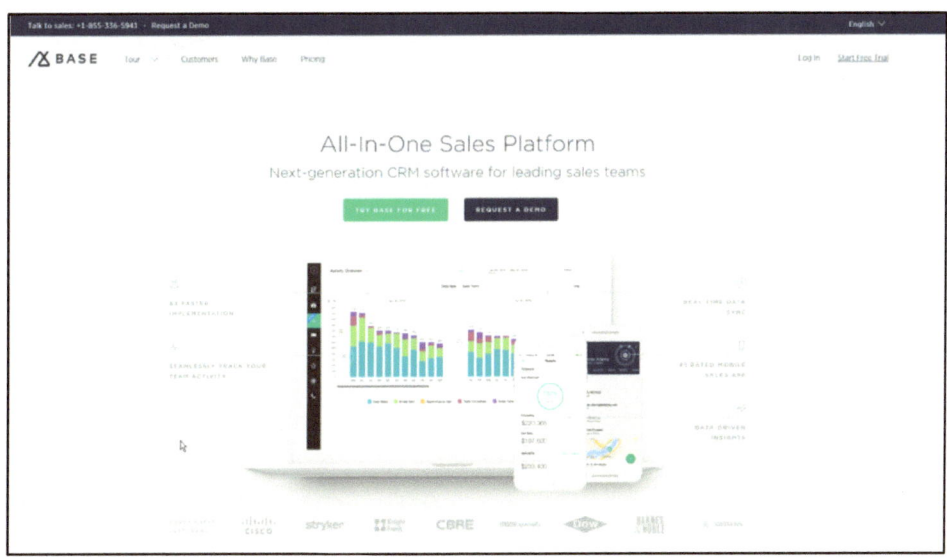

HubSpotCRM https://www.hubspot.com/products/crm

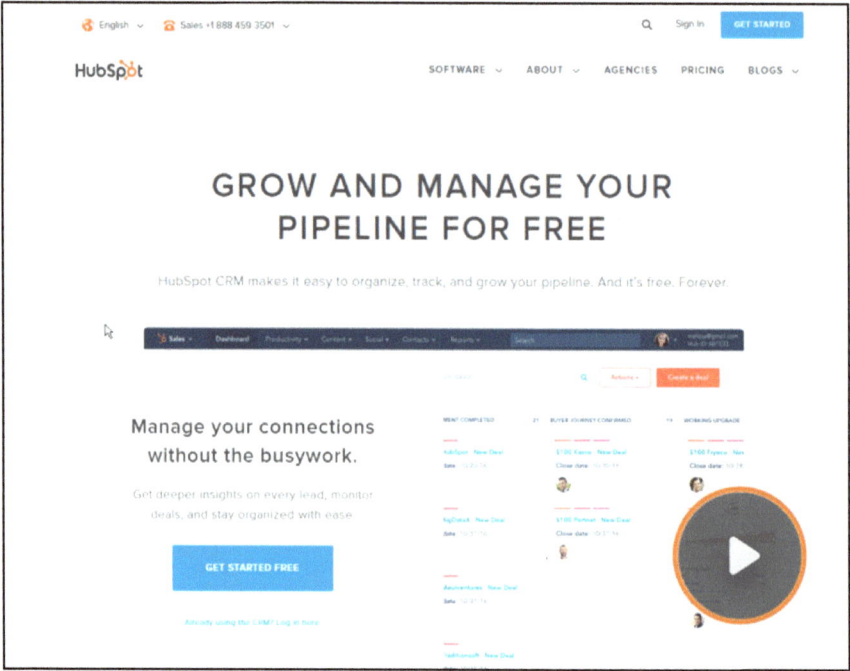

Cloud Only

Freshsales https://www.freshsales.io

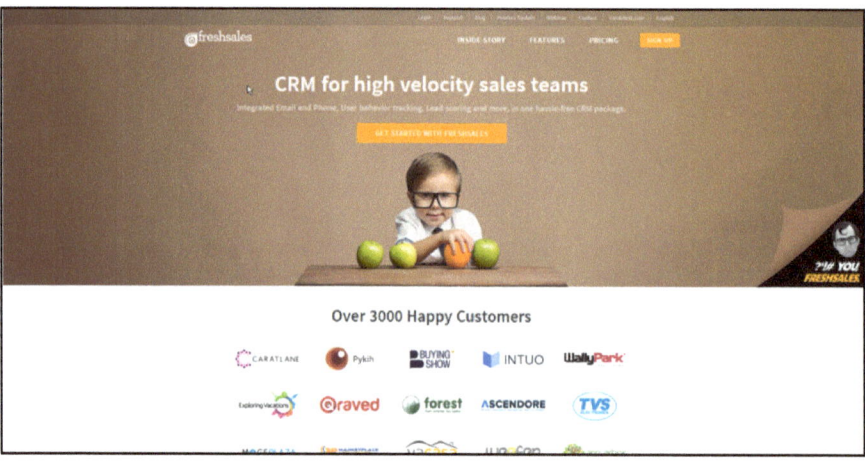

All of these CRM Software programs offer you a free trial for about 30-45 days, so you can decide which program is best for you.

Using a CRM System

Once you choose your CRM system and set it up, use it as a daily guide for what you are going to do each day, enter each new contact you meet, and ote how and when you plan to follow up. As you get other leads and referrals from a follow-up meeting, phone conversation, or email, enter those in your CRM system, too.

If you are collecting a lot of business cards at a meeting or event, there may be too many to enter in the CRM, such as if you collect all the cards from a display at a Chamber of Commerce office or if several dozen people pass their cards around at a business networking group meeting. Perhaps stick most of these cards in a box for further processing, but add the ones which are potential leads or referrals and add those to your CRM system. This way you select the potential buyers or individuals of influence who might be a source of leads and referrals for you.

Then, take those cards you have identified as people to contact – your PTC group, and enter them into your CRM system. Once entered, rate them in terms of their likelihood to be buyers (1-5 as previously noted) or to be a good source of referrals to prospective customers or clients (1-5 as also noted).

You can follow-up using the phone call or email to set up a meeting or more extended phone conversation to pitch your product. Then, enter the follow-up call or email, the date of the meeting, and any further notes on what approach to use in the future.

Because of all the detail you are entering, use your CRM like a daily, weekly, and monthly calendar to keep track of what you do. Later, you can use the accumulating stats for your daily, weekly, and monthly activities as a guide to your usual pattern of activities and what approaches are working the best.

For example, tally up the number of prospects or connections who you contacted by email or phone and note the number of each type of contact that led to a sale. Then, do more follow-up with the individuals in that category. For instance, if your emails are leading to the most meetings which result in the most sales, continue to do that. But if your phone follow-ups produce better results, use that approach. Or if you are doing both – sending an email and following up with a phone call – or making a call and confirming with an email – continue to do both.

In any event, seek to set up a meeting with a likely prospect or connection as soon as possible after you first meet, since you and your contact will better remember your exchange at the meeting, and the person will appreciate your responsiveness, which adds to your credibility. In some cases, you may be able to schedule a future meeting at a meeting, where you and the other party both whip out your calendars to set the date, time, and location.

After you set up a meeting, send a reminder a day or two before to confirm that you are still having this meeting. Also, set a reminder to send a follow-up thank you after the meeting. In this follow up, you might comment on how much you enjoyed the meeting and found it helpful, or you might point up the highlights of what the meeting accomplished. Such information not only increases your credibility and authority, it helps you and the other party know where you are in the deal discussion process, which can help you close the deal. It can also help you make an immediate or future sale, because your conversation at the event will be better remembered; it will have more emotional energy because it is still recent and seems more urgent to further discuss the possibilities. Still, you can later follow up after several weeks by explaining the reason for the delay in a positive way, such as you were involved in looking for the best, new products.

Finally, use the CRM system as a guide or reminder for what you are doing the next day, week, or month. In this way, you can better plan what you are doing each day and control your time. As they say: "You have to control your time to control the results," or conversely, "If you are not in control of your time, you are not in control of the results."

To use the CRM system as a guide and keep what you are doing top of mind, review your next day's activities the night before. This is also a good time to do a quick review of what is coming in the next week or weeks. Then, by knowing what is happening the following day, you can get everything ready the night before or first thing in the morning, so you can be well prepared for any meetings. Also, if you have to make any phone calls or send any emails, you can check when you are doing this and how much time you have allotted for this activity.

ABOUT THE AUTHOR

GINI GRAHAM SCOTT, Ph.D., J.D., is a nationally known writer, consultant, speaker, and seminar leader, specializing in business and work relationships, professional and personal development, social trends, and popular culture. She has published over 50 books with major publishers. She has worked with dozens of clients on memoirs, self-help, popular business books, and film scripts. Writing samples are at www.ginigrahamscott.com and www.changemakerspublishingandwriting.com. She is a Huffington Post regular columnist, commenting on social trends, business, and everyday life at www.huffingtonpost.com/gini-graham-scott.

She is the founder of Changemakers Publishing, featuring books on work, business, psychology, social trends, and self-help. It has published over 50 print, e-books, and audiobooks. She has licensed several dozen books for foreign sales, including the UK, Russia, Korea, Spain, and Japan.

She has received national media exposure for her books, including appearances on *Good Morning America, Oprah,* and *CNN*. She has been the producer and host of a talk show series, *Changemakers*, featuring interviews on social trends.

Her books on business relationships and professional development include:

Turn Your Dreams into Reality (Llewellyn)
Resolving Conflict (Changemakers Publishing)
A Survival Guide for Working with Bad Bosses (AMACOM)
A Survival Guide for Working with Humans (AMACOM)
Credit Card Fraud with Jen Grondahl Lee (Rowman)
Lies and Liars: How and Why Sociopaths Lie (Skyhorse Publishing)

Scott is also active in a number of community and business groups, including the Lafayette, Pleasant Hill, and Danville Chambers of Commerce. She is a graduate of the prestigious Leadership Contra Costa program, is a member of two B2B groups in Danville and Walnut Creek, and a BNI member. She is the organizer of six Meetup groups in the film and publishing industries with over 5000 members in Los Angeles and the San Francisco Bay Area. She does workshops and seminars on the topics of her books.

She received her Ph.D. from the University of California, Berkeley, and her J.D. from the University of San Francisco Law School. She has received several MAs at Cal State University, East Bay.

CHANGEMAKERS PUBLISHING

3527 Mt. Diablo Blvd., #273

Lafayette, CA 94549

changemakers@pacbell.net . (925) 385-0608

www.changemakerspublishingandwriting.com

www.ingramcontent.com/pod-product-compliance
Lightning Source LLC
Chambersburg PA
CBHW041303180526
45172CB00003B/942